-ash as in trash

Pam Scheunemann

Consulting Editor Monica Marx, M.A./Reading Specialist

ABDO
Publishing Company

Published by SandCastle™, an imprint of ABDO Publishing Company, 4940 Viking Drive, Edina, Minnesota 55435.

Printed in the United States.

Credits
Edited by: Pam Price
Curriculum Coordinator: Nancy Tuminelly
Cover and Interior Design and Production: Mighty Media
Photo Credits: BananaStock Ltd., Brand X Pictures, Comstock, Corbis Images, Digital Vision, Hemera, PhotoDisc, Rubberball Productions, Stockbyte

Library of Congress Cataloging-in-Publication Data

Scheunemann, Pam, 1955-
     -Ash as in trash / Pam Scheunemann.
        p. cm. -- (Word families. Set VI)
     Summary: Introduces, in brief text and illustrations, the use of the letter combination "ash" in such words as "trash," "rash," "dash," and "splash."
     ISBN 1-59197-260-4
     1. Readers (Primary) [1. Vocabulary. 2. Reading.] I. Title.

PE1119 .S2342147 2003
428.1--dc21   2002038224

SandCastle™ books are created by a professional team of educators, reading specialists, and content developers around five essential components that include phonemic awareness, phonics, vocabulary, text comprehension, and fluency. All books are written, reviewed, and leveled for guided reading, early intervention reading, and Accelerated Reader® programs and designed for use in shared, guided, and independent reading and writing activities to support a balanced approach to literacy instruction.

Let Us Know

After reading the book, SandCastle would like you to tell us your stories about reading. What is your favorite page? Was there something hard that you needed help with? Share the ups and downs of learning to read. We want to hear from you! To get posted on the ABDO Publishing Company Web site, send us e-mail at:

sandcastle@abdopub.com

SandCastle Level: Beginning

-ash Words

cash

flash

sash

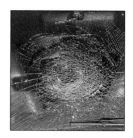

smash

splash

trash

Lee has a tray of cash.

Each of the cameras
has a **flash**.

Joe's dad wore a sash.

The glass was broken in a smash.

Jack made a big
splash.

Mr. Jones dropped the
trash.

Mr. Nash's Big Bash

There was a man
named Mr. Nash.

He decided
to throw a
great big bash.

12

13

He invited Fred,
who wore a sash.

Ed came as Mr. Flash.

Mr. Nash
had a piñata
for us to smash.

There was also a pool
in which to splash.

Tad took photos
without a flash.

Then Mr. Nash
handed out cash!

At the end
of the bash,
Ned took out
the trash.

The -ash Word Family

ash	lash
bash	mash
cash	Mr. Nash
crash	rash
dash	sash
flash	smash
gash	splash
hash	trash

Glossary

Some of the words in this list may have more than one meaning. The meaning listed here reflects the way the word is used in the book.

bash   a large party

flash   a device used to make a short burst of very bright light while taking a picture

piñata   a brightly decorated container filled with candy and gifts that children break open by hitting it with a stick while blindfolded

sash   a band of fabric tied around the waist or worn over the shoulder as decoration or part of a uniform

About SandCastle™

A professional team of educators, reading specialists, and content developers created the SandCastle™ series to support young readers as they develop reading skills and strategies and increase their general knowledge. The SandCastle™ series has four levels that correspond to early literacy development in young children. The levels are provided to help teachers and parents select the appropriate books for young readers.

Emerging Readers
(no flags)

Beginning Readers
(1 flag)

Transitional Readers
(2 flags)

Fluent Readers
(3 flags)

These levels are meant only as a guide. All levels are subject to change.

To see a complete list of SandCastle™ books and other nonfiction titles from ABDO Publishing Company, visit www.abdopub.com or contact us at:

4940 Viking Drive, Edina, Minnesota 55435 • 1-800-800-1312 • fax: 1-952-831-1632